The Dark Secret of HRD

Four Things You Need to Know to Stop Wasting Money on Training

Dennis E. Coates, Ph.D.

Published under the copyright laws of the Library of Congress of The United States of America by:

Performance Support Systems, Inc.
P.O. Box 1655
Newport News, VA 23601
TOLL-FREE – 800-488-6463
LOCAL – 757-873-3700
FAX – 757-873-3288
WEB – www.StrongForPerformance.com
EMAIL – info@prostarcoach.com

CONTENTS

Executive Summary

The purpose of this document is to inform you about four poorly understood realities related to employee performance. The failure to acknowledge them has caused organizations in the U.S. to waste nearly $100 billion every year on learning and development programs that fail to change behavior. The book explains why this horrible condition has persisted for decades, and what to do to get maximum ROI from an investment in learning programs.

REALITY #1: Most of the money invested in learning and development is wasted. This is what I call the "dark secret of HRD." Organizations that invest in training aren't getting what they paid for. Not even close. The reason is that knowing what to do isn't at all the same thing as doing it. In the long run, what people learn about in training usually isn't applied in the workplace. This failure to translate classroom instruction to workplace performance has been on the street for a long time, but for various reasons the message hasn't reached top management.

REALITY #2: At work, people usually don't think about how to act; instead, they automatically engage ingrained work habits. In a typical workplace, there's a lot going on and employees have a lot to think about. Under pressure, habits trump newly introduced skills. This reality is a formidable "catch-22"– most of the time, people won't use a newly learned skill until it's ingrained. But they usually don't make a conscious effort to exercise it because it's easier to rely on what's already habitual.

REALITY #3: To ingrain a work habit, people have to rewire their brains—they have to apply the skill consistently and repeatedly until the brain cells related to the skill interconnect into a new circuit, a process that takes far more time than is available in a training program. This is the biggest reason training programs don't "stick," why eight or nine out of ten participants don't improve their work habits. The most important part of training has to take place in the workplace—after classroom instruction is over.

The failure to follow through with a structured, long-term program of reinforcement means that most participants will return to their old work habits.

REALITY #4: Employees need people skills and personal strengths to work at their best. Even if employees apply what they learned in training, they still may not be able to give the high level of effort managers seek. The reason is that if they lack key people skills or have deficits in personal strength, they'll act inappropriately with each other and with customers. And they won't do the hard things when faced with challenges and adversity.

As you read through *The Dark Secret*, you'll learn a few things you didn't know about the brain. I've been studying cognitive neuroscience for over 20 years, and in this book I include a few important insights about "the learning instrument"—the human brain. It's important to know how the brain learns new skills, habits and patterns; otherwise you won't appreciate why you need to do what's necessary to get people to change their behavior. Understanding how people learn is the first step to avoid pouring big bucks down a hole.

But knowing these things is only the beginning and actually doesn't make a learning professional's job any easier. The commonsense remedies are daunting—which may be why few organizations have implemented them.

The book finishes on a positive note. In the final chapters I explain why and how we developed *Strong for Performance*, a unique online coaching and development system that essentially resolves the four issues that hold people back from getting the results executives expect when they invest in training.

Dennis E. Coates, Ph.D. – 2014

Chapter 1

How We Got into the Training Business—And Why We Got Out

I graduated from the U.S. Military Academy at West Point in 1967, and 20 years later I retired from the U.S. Army as a lieutenant colonel. Like most of my military colleagues, my job had been to help soldiers get better at doing difficult tasks under difficult conditions. This wasn't easy, and I wanted to know what worked, what didn't, and why. I read a lot of books about learning, performance and leadership. And I attended a lot of courses.

My learning journey continued after I retired and started my consulting business, Performance Support Systems, Inc. Today, well into the 21st century, I'm still learning.

Not everyone aims to achieve

One thing I've learned over and over as a small business entrepreneur is that most things worth doing are hard. It's hard to get people to contribute their best work and to cooperate as a team. It's hard to go against the grain and create a new product. It's hard to compete in the marketplace. It's hard to deal with the surprises that come up in any given business week. It's hard to survive the downturns in the economy.

And not just for business owners and top managers. It's hard for everybody who's trying to find a good job, succeed in it, have a family and enjoy life. The myriad challenges that people have to deal with are mind-boggling.

I've always been fascinated with why certain people strive, achieve and succeed—and others don't. Why are some people life-long learners, while others roll their eyes at the idea of self-improvement?

For many, the world of work is a dreary aspect of life, and not everyone is striving and achieving on a path to success. Some people don't make good career choices, and they end up in jobs they don't like. Some people don't work well with others. Some lack perspective. Others aren't motivated to learn. Many aren't inclined to give their best work every day. They dislike their bosses and do only what they're told to do. And even then, they don't do it very well. In tough times, they get laid off. Afterwards, to get by, they end up doing work they like even less.

I've also come to accept that not all business executives feel it's important to develop their people. Maybe they don't believe that to get results, managers have to lead. Maybe they don't appreciate how learning works or what it takes for an employee to change a work habit. Maybe they feel that investing in learning and development won't make much difference, and that money is more wisely invested elsewhere.

The early years – training and consulting

For about 25 years now, my company has been focused on these issues. I've read nearly a thousand business books and have applied what I learned, both to make my business strong and to create products and services that make a difference. In 1987 we created *MindFrames,* a personality assessment based on cognitive neuroscience. In 1994 we introduced *20/20 Insight*, a breakthrough performance feedback system. It was a new approach because it put the survey process in the hands of the learning professionals, which reduced costs by an order of magnitude. It was self-customizable, so they could locally validate surveys and administer them to everyone in the organization—not just to upper-level managers. It also let them administer more than a dozen different kinds of surveys on one platform.

And in 2013 we introduced *Strong for Performance*, a 24/7 online virtual coaching system that supports the learning of core skills and reinforces development over time—until skills become ingrained habits.

And of course all this experience has taught me some interesting lessons.

One lesson is that our market—our base of potential customers—is success-oriented people. It's people who want to continue learning, growing and improving themselves. Also, the organizations that buy our products are those that value employee development. Even though we'll never stop doing all we can to educate people about what it takes to improve, achieve and succeed, we know that our products are for people and organizations that "get it."

In the early years of Performance Support Systems, we were a management consulting company. Our strength was designing and delivering customized training. We never used off-the-shelf programs. We always felt our content was better, and to meet our clients' needs we created programs especially for them. It was what we did best.

But the danger is that to a hammer, every problem can look like a nail.

Training isn't always the solution

We might have made this classic mistake, except for a key insight I discovered in the early 1980s, a few years before I retired from the Army. I was assigned to the U.S. Army Training Board at Fort Eustis, Virginia. The Board was a kind of "think tank" for developing concepts and products to improve the way the Army trains soldiers. As a project manager, my job was to coordinate the development of a program called "Battalion Training Management System" (BTMS) and train the trainers at units worldwide.

To prepare myself, I observed the training at most of the major Army installations in the U.S. I attended several courses and read widely about training design and development. The most profound thing I learned was that *if people are performing poorly, it's not always a training problem*. This insight is embedded in a book by Robert Mager and Peter Pipe, called *Analyzing Performance Problems*.

The principle is one of the few "great ideas" in learning and development to come along in the past 50 years. Previously, most executives assumed that if people weren't performing up to par, they needed more training. The essence of Mager and Pipe's insight is that the problem may lie in any or all of these three general areas.

1. First, **people may not know how**. They may lack the required skills, knowledge or experience. If this is the case, they need training. Or, if the task is procedural, maybe a simple job aid will do.

2. On the other hand, **they may not want to**. They may not value the activity or feel it's important. Or it may not be interesting to them. Doing the work may not meet their needs. In this case, the solution is motivation, which comes from within. Leaders need to inspire them by relating the work to what drives them—their needs, values, goals, attitudes, and interests.

3. Finally, they ***may not have what they need*** to do their best work. They may know how, and they may feel motivated, but they may lack authority, guidance, information, personnel, facilities, supplies, tools, technology, transportation, funds, and other resources. Since virtually all these things must be given to them by their organization, people rely on their managers for empowerment.

These guidelines sound simple enough. Training is expensive, and it's a mistake to invest in it if the problem lies elsewhere. After you've paid for training design, materials, technology, services, facilities, and the opportunity cost of taking participants away from their work, pretty soon you're talking *real money*. Not to mention the ill will you get when you make people go to training when they don't need it. And if the problem isn't a lack of know-how, you'll still have a performance shortfall after the training program is over.

The solution becomes the problem

Yes, performance analysis is a fundamental concept, but after the experts and bureaucrats got through with it, their guidelines were so complex that they were hard to follow. For example, the Air Force's version of Instructional System Design (ISD) was packaged in three huge volumes. You could paper the walls with the flow charts describing the process. Even Mager and Pipe's simpler approach came in a boxed set of five books. You had to be an expert to understand what the gurus were recommending.

And since management couldn't make heads or tails of it, they had to trust the experts to decipher and implement this convoluted process, which in itself was shockingly time-consuming and expensive. ISD had a kind of logic to it, but if you followed it to the letter, you could go out of business before you figured out what to do about your performance problem. Still, a lot of trainers who convinced their organizations of the wisdom of doing all this earned quite a meal ticket for themselves.

This is probably why you don't hear much about ISD anymore. But Mager and Pipe's basic insight remains a valid and useful guideline.

At Performance Support Systems, we didn't recommend training when we knew the problem lay elsewhere. However, we discovered that sometimes our clients insisted on training regardless of what the real problem was. When we suggested that we do some front-end analysis to verify whether training was needed, they objected that it was unnecessary and they didn't want to spend the money for it. Often the message was, "We want the training. If you don't want to do the work, we'll find someone else."

In the 1980s, spurred by Japanese competition, the U.S. was swept up in the quality movement. A training solution called Total Quality Management (TQM) was adopted by HR departments everywhere. Thousands of consultants delivered billions of dollars of TQM training, whether it was needed or not. Executives wanted to be able to say they were addressing the quality issue head-on, and as proof they pointed to all the TQM courses that had been delivered.

This political approach to training put consultants in an awkward position. We were good at delivering training. So when potential clients demanded it, did we turn away business or did we give them what they asked for? If we accepted the work, we'd maintain a positive cash flow. But if what was holding the organization back wasn't a training problem, down the road our clients wouldn't be happy about the result, and we could be blamed for it.

Did we accept the work anyway? In the beginning, yes, we sometimes did. But there was no heart in projects like this, and before long we decided to get out of the training services business. Instead, we began developing and marketing performance improvement products.

The dark secret – most training doesn't "stick"

Insisting on training when competence wasn't the issue wasn't the only problem. It wasn't even the biggest problem. Not by a long shot. Something else was going on that caused organizations to waste billions—no, *tens* of billions of dollars every year on programs that didn't get the desired results. No one realized what was going on, and to this day most organizations still don't.

I remember the exact moment when I decided to get out of the training business. It happened over 20 years ago as I was having lunch with a colleague in a restaurant south of Chicago. We had just spent the morning with the vice president for human resources at one of the biggest corporations in the U.S. We were reviewing what was said and what we learned. At some point, I looked at him over my cup of coffee. It was one of those moments when I felt that it was important to be honest.

I said, "You know, Chris, whatever you do they probably won't get the results you expect, or what they think they're paying for. I'm not saying you're a second-rate trainer. Quite the opposite. You're probably the best trainer I know. But I honestly don't think your program will change anything."

He sat up straight and looked at me with a puzzled expression. "What are you talking about?"

"What I'm saying is, it's rare that this kind of training has the impact it's supposed to. I don't know how many times we've analyzed their needs and then given the client our best stuff, promised a lot, delivered more and gotten rave reviews. Then a year or two later, when we went back to talk with the managers, they told us that practically nothing had changed. It's frustrating and disappointing to admit that what we do doesn't really have much long-term impact. Surely, you've experienced the same thing."

He looked out the window and didn't say anything. I thought I might have hurt his feelings. Maybe I shouldn't have said what I was thinking.

But then he said, "I suppose you're right. Yes, I've been disappointed like that. Yes, probably most of the time. But what are we supposed to do? Stop trying? Get into another line of work? Besides, even if the training doesn't take with everyone, there's always those few who take it to heart. It helps those few. And the rest, well, if their behavior doesn't change, maybe their thinking does. Maybe it has an impact down the road."

"I don't know if that's good enough, Chris. Companies large and small are spending a ton of money every year to hire people like you and me to improve the skills of their employees. That's the ROI they expect, but it's not what they're getting. The training doesn't stick. It's like some kind of deep dark secret that nobody wants to talk about. The thing is, I know it and you know it. It makes me feel conflicted and uncomfortable with this business."

"So what are you going to do? Stop training? What?"

"I don't know. I've been thinking about writing an article about this problem. I have an outline..."

"Oh no, man, don't write it. A negative article like that, if anybody published it, and if anybody read it, would hurt our efforts to get organizations to invest in their people. It would be bad for all of us. People would come after you. It's a bad idea, Denny. Don't do it."

I wanted to do it, though. I kept thinking about all that wasted investment, all that effort for very little gain.

But I never did write the "dark secret" article.

Why not? I think basically I didn't want to be someone who raises an ugly issue without giving a good explanation for it or without proposing some kind of solution. And to this day, organizations world-wide still invest tens of billions of dollars annually in instruction that fails to produce lasting changes in behavior and improved workplace performance.

The good news is, I eventually came to understand why most training doesn't "stick." I even learned what to do about it.

Chapter 2

Reality #1 – The Dark Secret Is Exposed

Myth #1

When employees have skill deficits, invest in the best training you can find, and your performance problems will be "fixed."

I never had to write my "dark secret" article. I discovered that a number of learning experts had already noticed the same "transfer of training" problem, and quite a few articles about it had already showed up in professional journals.

What the experts were saying

Perhaps the earliest of these was "Why Training Programs Fail to Carry Over," published by James Mosel in 1957 in *Personnel*. He referred to "mounting evidence that shows that very often the training makes little or no difference in job behavior."

In 1988 Timothy Baldwin and Kevin Ford published "Transfer of Training: A Review and Directions for Future Research" in *Personnel Psychology*. They reviewed all the research to date and concluded that "there is a growing recognition of a 'transfer problem' in organizational training today. It is estimated that while American industries annually spend up to $100 billion on training and development, not more than 10% of these expenditures actually result in transfer to the job."

After the articles came the books. Their common theme: ***instruction nearly always fails to translate to improved performance in the workplace.*** The authors claimed that while managers willingly invest millions in training, they typically refuse to invest in the necessary follow-through effort to ingrain what was learned. Most of these books explain what the author believes an effective follow-through should look like.

The first book was *Transfer of Training: Action-Packed Strategies to Ensure High Payoff from Training Investments* (1992), by Mary L. Broad and John W. Newstrom. Their premise: "Most of [the] investment in organizational training and development is wasted because most of the knowledge and skills gained in training (well over 80%, by some estimates) is not fully applied by those employees on the job." She states that "improving transfer of training must become HRD's top priority" and describes over 60 actions organizations can take before, during and after training that will correct the problem. But this exhaustive collection of strategies didn't add up to a strategy that organizations could follow, and nearly 20 years later, we know that Broad's call to action was never taken to heart.

What followed was a stream of books offering varying solutions to the transfer of training problem:

- Mary Broad and Jack Phillips, *Transferring Learning to the Workplace* (1997)
- Jeffrey Pfeffer and Robert I. Sutton, *The Knowing-Doing Gap: How Smart Companies Turn Knowledge into Action* (2000)
- Robert Brinkerhoff and Anne Apking, *High Impact Learning: Strategies for*

Leveraging Business Results from Training (2001)

- Mary Broad, *Beyond Transfer of Training: Engaging Systems to Improve Performance* (2005)
- Donald Kirkpatrick and James Kirkpatrick, *Transferring Learning to Behavior* (2005)
- Calhoun Wick *et al*, *The Six Disciplines of Breakthrough Learning* (2006)

One after the other, these books repeated this appalling fact:

Reality #1

Without months of follow-through reinforcement, application, feedback, encouragement and accountability, as much as 90% of all classroom instruction doesn't "stick" in the workplace. Because of the failure to follow through, $50-$100 billion is wasted every year in the U.S. alone.

Top management is kept in the dark

Unfortunately, this message has failed to grab the attention of top management. The dark secret has remained dark all these years. I believe there are several reasons for this:

- These aren't the kind of business books that top managers read. These books are targeted at HR executives. And if HR executives noticed any of them, the message is now "old news." The dire warnings have been overtaken by a new wave of HR flavors of the month, such as "emotional intelligence," "engagement," "learning management systems" and "talent management systems."
- Maybe the message seems alarmist—too awful to be true.
- The authors aren't singing from the same page of the hymnal. Yes, they all have religion, but each is singing a different song, presumably the one that favors their business focus. Consequently, they don't promote a single, compelling solution.

- While most of the books assert that a structured program of follow-through is needed, none of them explains *why* this is the solution. It's unlikely that any CEO will support the additional expense of follow-through without justification.
- The solutions offered by the authors are either too general or too focused on their own limited HRD specialty to add up to a successful strategy. So what's a well-intentioned executive to do?

It's unlikely that an HR executive will study all the books, consolidate all the recommendations into a practical strategy, and present it to the CEO, especially if it means overhauling the HR culture.

But there are credible reasons why a structured program of long-term follow-through will always be needed, and there's a practical way to set it up.

Chapter 3

Reality #2 – How Work Habits Are Created: The Message from Brain Science

Myth #2:

If people value what they learned in training, they'll do it on the job.

For over 20 years I've been reading about cognitive neuroscience, a passionate interest that took hold as I developed a brain-based personality assessment now known as *MindFrames*.

How I became passionately interested in the brain

I believe that personality has an impact on behavior. The more you're aware of your behavioral tendencies, the better you can manage them. With this kind of self-awareness you can consciously choose to emphasize your strengths. You can also choose to stretch out of your comfort zone when you need to do the uncomfortable things that are required for success.

After studying the most widely used personality assessments, I concluded that they weren't reliable enough or sufficiently grounded in science to use with my clients. Personality originates in the brain, so ideally any model and measurement of personality should be consistent with the latest cognitive neuroscience. And this was simply not the case with any of the established assessments. So I decided to develop my own instrument, based on brain science.

If I had known then how much work this would entail, I probably wouldn't have pursued it. It has taken 20 years of research, development and testing to achieve what I wanted.

But what's important is that along the way I gained some crucial insights about conscious awareness, memory and learning. I discovered what's really happening in the brain when people learn a new skill or improve a work habit—the behavior patterns that matter in the workplace.

When attention is challenged, ingrained habits take over

One huge insight I learned about the brain is that it can do many things at once. Certainly you have more than one thing going on in your work, not to mention your life. So it's a good thing that your brain does a lot of parallel processing. It has over 100 complex areas that interact all day long. Some of this work happens consciously. Most of it happens outside of conscious awareness.

Here's what I learned, and it's terribly important: You can consciously pay attention to only one of these thought processes at a time.

This may sound like a crippling limitation, but actually your survival depends on your inability to take in everything at once. Imagine, if you can, what it would be like to be in an elevator, consciously remembering a sunset on a dock while analyzing your plans for a project as you listen to the lyrics of the song in the elevator while being aware of how your clothes feel a little too confining on your body and the ache in your legs from jogging the day before—all this while paying attention to what your associate is telling you on the way to the 10th floor.

No way. You can't pay attention to all of it. If that were possible, your conscious awareness would be flooded with too much information all at once. You would be overwhelmed by the chaos of all that input. You wouldn't be able to consciously process it all or make effective decisions. No, it's a good thing you can't do it.

What you **can** do is consciously **shift** from one area of brain activity to another—even quickly back and forth. But to think clearly about something, you need to be able to focus on one thing at a time.

The other night I was driving home from my health club. As I neared my neighborhood, I was thinking about some ideas I got while sitting in the hot tub. I was so intensely focused on this that I thought the traffic light at the intersection I was approaching was the one in front of the elementary school. But no, it was the intersection a mile past it, the entrance to my community! I had driven by the school without being aware of it! I snapped out of my mental wanderings quickly enough to realize where I was and safely make my turn.

This wasn't the first time I've been caught day-dreaming at the wheel. I've been known to miss a turn or two. I'm sure it's the kind of thing that happens to most people.

Have you ever chatted with someone interesting at a social gathering and in the middle of the conversation heard your name mentioned not far away? If so, you know what happened next. Your attention shifted to that area of the room to hear the rest of what they were saying about you. During the seconds while your attention was focused somewhere else, you didn't hear what your conversation partner was saying. You momentarily "blanked out" while your attention was somewhere else, and you had to say, "Ginger, forgive me, but could you say that last part again?"

Maybe something like this has happened while you were reading the paper at breakfast and the person across from you tried to tell you something. You had to stop reading to hear the message, or you decided to disregard it and continue reading. You couldn't take in both simultaneously.

I'm talking about a physical, biological limitation: ***You can shift your attention back and forth, but you can't pay attention to two things at the same time.***

To use a skill in a busy workplace, it has to become a habit

This is why ingraining a skill is so important. After the brain cells that enable a particular skill have been connected into a neural pathway circuit, you don't have to pay attention to the activity to do it! After thousands of hours of hitting baseballs, a player doesn't have to pay attention to how he swings the bat. He can focus his attention on how the pitcher is releasing the ball. After countless repetitions of effective listening skills, you don't have to pay attention to the basic steps. You can just focus on understanding what the person is saying.

Reality #2

Until a new skill has been ingrained, people have to concentrate to do it right. In a busy workplace, conscious awareness is quickly filled to capacity. So until a new skill becomes an unconscious work habit, old habits will prevail most of the time. Repeated failures to apply the new skill can be discouraging, and people

typically go back to their old, previously ingrained patterns.

This is one of the reasons why most people who return from training eventually lapse into their old patterns. Without a structured program of ongoing reinforcement, application, feedback, encouragement and accountability to help them apply what they learned, the skills won't become habitual. People know what they should be doing, but when their brains are filled with the fast-paced and high-pressured activity of a typical workplace, it's hard to concentrate long enough to apply a newly learned behavior pattern. It's far easier to let old, ingrained patterns do their work. After a few failures to implement what they learned, most people are discouraged enough to give up.

Given this reality, the all-important question is, what does it take to ingrain a skill? The answer will shock you.

Chapter 4

Reality #3 – What Brain Science Says about Changing Work Habits

Myth #3

If motivated people learn what to do in training, they'll begin using the desired skills consistently after they return to work.

Discovering how the brain learns new patterns was momentous for me. It led me to understand **why** the post-training follow-through is absolutely essential. It's because what people take away from the classroom is mainly knowledge and familiarity, not skill.

There's simply not enough time in any training course to provide for enough repetitions that will cause the brain to wire itself for a work habit.

How a skill becomes a habit

In the best-case training scenario, skills are *introduced* in the classroom along with enough role-play practice to *familiarize* participants with the model.

The practice that leads to ingraining the skill has to happen after people return to work.

Behavior patterns become second nature only after the brain cells involved have interconnected to form a neural pathway.

How does this happen?

The first thing you need to understand is that from the perspective of your brain, skills, practices, execution, routines, and habits are all the same thing—behavior patterns.

A behavior pattern is a consistently repeated series of mental and physical actions. Perceptions may lead to feelings and thoughts, and then to a decision and finally to a series of coordinated actions. Specific brain cells— sometimes groups of brain cells—are involved in these actions. Once all the related brain cells are physically interconnected in a neural pathway, you have an efficient circuit for triggering the appropriate response—whether consciously or unconsciously. You can do what you need to do efficiently and without having to think about it.

A work habit doesn't mean you can't consciously decide to do something else. You can think, "Well, in this situation I usually do this. But based on what's going on, this time I'll do something else instead."

What causes the brain cells to interconnect?

The answer—repetitions of the desired behavior. As athletic coaches are fond of saying—practice, practice, and more practice. The ultimate goal is to make the series of actions habitual—an ingrained behavior pattern.

Habits are more important than most people realize. Can you imagine waking up every morning having to figure out all over again how to do every little thing—brush your teeth, tie your shoes, make coffee, and drive a car? If your brain couldn't form habits, if all day long you had to consciously decide every single action, you probably wouldn't be able to survive. The mode that favors survival is habit—unconscious, automatic execution of routine behavior.

Here's how it happens. With each repetition of the desired action, the brain cells involved are stimulated to grow dendrites, tiny filaments on the brain cell. Eventually these filaments connect the related brain cells with each other. The result is a neural pathway that efficiently, unconsciously enables the desired behavior. Once the network is in place, you can do the action without thinking about it.

This process is familiar to anyone who has tried to master a skill or change a habit. For example, if you've ever tried to master a sport skill, you know this is how it works. You can't succeed if you have to think about what you're doing during the heat of competition. And it takes a ton of practice to ingrain the skills.

The stages of habit formation

Experts in the field of behavior change talk about four stages.

The first stage is "unconscious incompetence." Initially, you may lack skill or have a bad habit— but you aren't aware that what you're doing is causing problems. Or you may be aware of it, but you don't appreciate how bad the consequences are. Or you may have decided that it's not worth the effort to make a change.

A person will remain in this state of unconscious incompetence until their pain, someone else's pain, or the appreciation of imminent failure convinces the individual that he should do something about it. Often the trigger is feedback.

The second stage is "conscious incompetence," when you recognize that the way you act is causing problems. You understand why what you're doing doesn't get you the results you want. This self-revelation can lead to trying something different. Often it causes a person to get coaching, study books or attend training courses.

Once you learn what you should be doing, you begin the third, most difficult stage—"conscious competence." This is the post-instruction phase. You try what you've learned, believing it will work better for you.

This is difficult because the new behavior isn't an ingrained habit yet. Without a fully connected neural pathway, you have to consciously work to make all the actions in the pattern happen. This requires concentration and effort—a lot of mental energy. So at first, during the flow of daily life and work, you may have a lot on your mind. Since it's not habitual, you may forget to do what you know you should do. Or maybe you do remember and consciously try to do it right, and your execution is awkward and ineffective.

Either way, you get frustrated. When you're trying hard and getting it wrong most of the time, you can get discouraged. Most people experience this in the earlier going, and much of the time they give up and return to their old way of doing things, which is already well-ingrained and comfortable.

Think about all those failed New Year's resolutions!

The key to success is to accept that failure is natural and inevitable and keep trying. If a person works through the discouragement and persists past the inevitable failures and frustrations, over time the "success rate" will slowly improve. The neurons will start to connect and the doing will become easier. What once felt awkward will start to feel familiar. Because the repetitions continue to stimulate the dendrites, the neural pathway will eventually complete itself—a physical circuit in the brain.

During all this frustration, the reinforcement, application, feedback, encouragement and accountability you get from coaching can make a huge difference.

If you persist long enough, you make it to the fourth and final stage: an ingrained habit. The enabling brain cells are all connected and competence has become habitual, meaning you can apply the skill or behavior pattern routinely without actually concentrating on doing it. You do it unconsciously, easily, and comfortably— "unconscious competence." At this stage, you "own" the skill. No matter how fast-paced or stressful your work may be, you can do the right thing automatically. All athletes know about the hard work of ingraining skills. It's no different in life or in the workplace.

Reality #3

To ingrain any skill, routine, habit or behavior pattern, you have to perform the correct action again and again to stimulate the brain cells

involved to interconnect. Only after the new neural network is established will someone consistently perform the skill on the job. Because of the time involved, this repetition can't happen in the classroom. It has to happen in the workplace.

Habits are formed in the workplace, not in training

This is why it's foolish to think that any training course—by itself, without months of structured follow-through reinforcement, application, feedback, encouragement and accountability—will change a person's behavior.

Even a two-week course can't come close to giving this much practice. Think about how many repetitions it takes to learn to do a speed turn in swimming, to execute a double play in less than two seconds, or to hit a golf ball out of a sand trap to within ten feet of the hole. But with enough practice, practice and more practice, the neural pathway will eventually be completely interconnected, and the new approach to behavior will seem effortless and automatic.

How much repetition? How long does it take? How patient and persistent does one have to be?

The simplest behavior patterns can take a month to ingrain, even if performed several times a day. More complex skills, such as interpersonal skills, will take longer, especially if they aren't applied in the workplace every day. Quite a lot of coaching is usually needed to help someone achieve unconscious competence.

But if you persist past all the discouragement, your success rate will improve. Ultimately, if you keep trying, the success rate will approach 100%. At this point, the doing of the new pattern will seem like an automatic habit. The skill will be ingrained, and it will be easy to perform it routinely on the job.

The all-important bottom line—*you can't use a skill consistently until it becomes an ingrained work habit.* It's true for athletes, and it's true for people in the workplace.

Even though these facts about behavior change and skill development are well-established, very few top managers know about them, which is why it's still rare for decision-makers to invest in an effective follow-up program. They don't appreciate that the role of training is to *introduce* the best practice, not to ingrain it. ***The real learning happens after classroom instruction is over.***

And this is why, to this day, tens of billions of training dollars are still being wasted every year.

Chapter 5

Reality #4 – No High Performance without Core Strengths

Myth #4

If you invest in training and follow-through reinforcement, and if people ingrain the business-related skills they learned in training, they will perform at a very high level.

Back in the days when our company provided management consulting services, one of my clients was an upscale retirement home. My job was to help the various units in the home work better as a team. During that year, I got to know the top management team. Towards the end of my assignment, the president decided to retire. This became the opportunity of a lifetime for the general manager, who had been grooming himself for this position for years. Unfortunately, he was not the person the board selected. A younger manager was promoted ahead of him, and the general manager resigned in anger.

As far as I could determine, it wasn't because he was a poor manager or didn't understand the business. He had plenty of experience in these areas. No, it was because he was distant and impersonal with the staff. In other words, he had poor *people skills*.

As everyone knows, the stock market tanked in 2007 when "the real estate bubble" burst. The market fell apart because a lot of high-level bank executives approved millions of high-risk mortgages. The fact that the lack of regulation allowed them to do it is beside the point. They were inattentive, reckless, irresponsible, unscrupulous and disloyal to their bank's stakeholders. Untold numbers of inappropriate loans defaulted and hundreds of banks were in danger of going out of business. Many did. Plus, millions of lives were devastated by the effects of the downturn.

This summary of what happened may be a little simplistic, but I think I got the gist of it right.

The point is, like the retirement home general manager, these guys really knew their business. They were highly educated, intelligent, and experienced in banking. They knew how to get things done. But that wasn't enough to keep them from running their corporations into the ground and wrecking the American economy in the process.

Their problem was that they lacked key *personal strengths*. They failed to do the hard things when it mattered.

At the core – people skills and personal strengths

I've seen similar scenarios played out hundreds of times in every kind of organization at all levels, from supervisors to chairmen of the board. It doesn't seem to matter who's involved. A person can have university degrees and years in the business, but if he or she has poor *people skills* or deficits of *personal strength*, none of this education or business acumen seems to matter. Bad things happen.

When evaluating employee performance, employers often miss crucial elements of ability. Whether conducting the interview, hiring the candidate, assigning the position, delivering the training, delegating the project, evaluating the results or making the promotion, management often fails to take something elemental into account. What they fail to give enough weight to is the core of a person's ability – the ability to interact effectively with people and the willingness to do the hard things when faced with adversity.

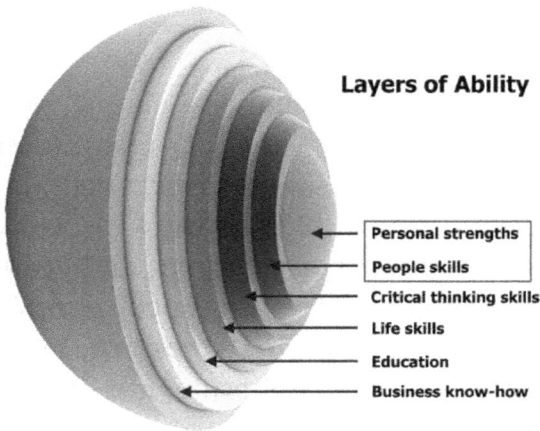

Layers of Ability

Personal strengths
People skills
Critical thinking skills
Life skills
Education
Business know-how

Does the person listen well? Resolve conflict? Ask for and receive feedback?

Most people don't have good *people skills*. Learning these skills in a systematic way has never been a part of formal education. Parents, teachers, coaches, ministers, mentors—even friends—influence what a child learns. In life, people learn how to get along through trial and error. As a result, some of these behavior patterns later cause problems in relationships and in the workplace. Recognizing their importance, many top executives try to make up for poor people skills by teaching them to managers, customer service people, and sales representatives.

A person may know the business, but is he trustworthy? Does he take initiative? Is he patient? Does he strive for excellence? Does he persevere? And so on. At the core of an individual's competence are several dozen *personal strengths*. While they're probably the most important behavior patterns a person can have, they're typically learned in a totally unconscious, haphazard way. The best opportunities for young people to gain personal strength are when they have to strive against adversity, such as dealing with hardship, participating in organized sports, and working their way through college. As important as personal strengths are to leadership and employee performance, these areas aren't addressed in developmental programs anywhere. It's hard to overemphasize the significance of this shortfall in education and professional development.

Reality #4

Ingrained business, management and technical skills aren't enough. To succeed in life and work, people skills and personal strengths are at the core.

Schools and universities can teach knowledge, and organizational training programs can teach business know-how, administrative procedures and management skills. But without effective people skills and personal strengths, people in the workplace will struggle to deliver the high levels of performance needed to achieve the results you expect.

Your parents didn't know this. Your coaches and mentors didn't know this. Your teachers and professors didn't know this. Certainly your friends didn't know this. Even your managers and trainers didn't know this.

But now *you* know this.

Chapter 6

People Skills Are Hard Skills, Not Soft Skills

Years ago, when Performance Support Systems was involved in management consulting, we created and implemented training programs to develop teams, improve call-center performance, help customer service personnel interact effectively with customers, train managers to lead, and teach sales representatives to build lasting relationships with clients.

We determined that the focus of all these programs had to be the same—people skills. As a result, we got very good at delivering training focused on improving these skills. This experience confirmed that most employees have a lot to learn about how to interact with people. We learned that it's rare for any individual to perform a people skill in the best way.

People skill development is neglected

This situation isn't surprising. As I mentioned previously, throughout one's formal education, it's rare for a people skill to be taught as a part of a curriculum.

I'm reminded of something that happened to me when I was on the faculty of the College of William and Mary. The dean put out a call for new course development. I was the head of the ROTC program there, and I taught the only leadership course available at the university. The students seem to value it; I had more non-ROTC students than cadets. So I wrote up a proposal for new courses in leadership development.

To my surprise, the dean told me this: "The purpose of a university is to acquire knowledge. It is not a fitting place to learn skills." I thought about the music, art and drama departments, but I didn't say anything. I just reflected on the fact that his attitude is part of the conventional wisdom, and that students would have to wait until they arrived at a workplace to learn these skills—if they were lucky.

It's when deficits in people skills threaten on-the-job success that organizations are motivated to invest in this type of training. Even so, it is still common for executives to refer to people skills as "soft skills," because they aren't about the specific business of the organization. They aren't about computers, vehicles, machines and other "hard" equipment. The perception is that getting along with people is nice, but "nice-to-have"—secondary to the operation of the business.

People skills are hard skills

Nothing is further from the truth. People skills are "hard" skills because in almost every job, they're crucial to workplace performance. They're at the core of every job in which contact with people is the main issue. If you don't work well with others, if you can't get things done through others, if you have trouble connecting with customers, all the education and business know-how in the world isn't going to make you effective.

For another thing, people skills are "hard skills" because they're hard to improve. People already have deeply ingrained behavioral patterns for most of the people skills. The problem is, they learned these habits "on the street." Consequently, the way they behave now often causes problems. They need to learn new patterns. This turns out to be harder than learning a brand new skill. When you try to improve the way a person performs a people skill, the new pattern has to compete with the old, comfortable pattern that's causing the problems. During the difficult period of "conscious competence," it's all too tempting to fall back on already-ingrained, dysfunctional ways of interacting with others.

Another problem that makes people skills hard to acquire is that the learning isn't well supported by books, videos and courses. I've read dozens of books on people skills, and the best of these focus on only a handful of key skills. Most books on leadership are written about and for high-level executives, not line managers, where leadership skills are essential. One key area of leadership skill involves coaching team members to perform at their best. But most books focus on mentoring and executive coaching, not skills for operational leaders. Video production companies treat only a few of the essential people skills, and their approach seems mostly to entertain and motivate, not to teach how.

One intellectual movement, called "emotional intelligence," introduced by Daniel Goleman over 15 years ago, shined a spotlight on people skills. But he aggregated people skills, managing emotions, personality and character traits into a single area of competence, further confusing the issue. The concept has become popular in some HR circles, which is unfortunate, because people skills have as much to do with logic as with emotions. Plus, this artificial clumping of important issues makes it easier for executives to segment "all that stuff" into a secondary "soft" area.

All the proponents of people skills fall short of describing the true scope of this element of workplace performance. If you ask consultants or trainers to name all the people skills, they're likely to name fewer than ten, certainly no more than fifteen.

But actually, there are several dozen essential people skills. These apply to all employees, whether managers or their direct reports:

- Communicate effectively in writing
- Defuse negative emotions

- Express feelings constructively
- Handle customer phone calls
- Interpret nonverbal behavior
- Listen to understand
- Facilitate dialogue
- Present a persuasive argument
- Request feedback
- Accept feedback
- Give positive feedback
- Give constructive feedback
- Request feedforward
- Give feedforward
- Affirm people's strengths
- Give encouragement
- Learn from experience
- Improve a work habit
- Set development goals
- Share information
- Express appreciation/gratitude
- Manage time
- Assert your needs
- Deal with difficult people
- Interact with diverse people
- Build rapport
- Build work relationships
- Show respect

- Apologize
- Accept apology
- Negotiate
- Avoid conflict
- Deal with complaints
- Ask for support
- Give support to coworkers
- Make a decision
- Resolve conflict
- Respond to a suggestion
- Solve problems
- Troubleshoot problems

There is also an impressive array of people skills that seem especially appropriate for managers who need to get results through people:

- Interview a candidate
- Respond to suggestions
- Give a briefing
- Give a speech
- Deal with behavior problems
- Teach a concept
- Teach a procedure

- Teach a skill
- Facilitate experiential learning
- Encourage constructive attitudes
- Assign roles and responsibilities
- Communicate vision
- Delegate responsibility
- Plan a strategy
- Set results goals
- Express expectations
- Empower people
- Give results feedback
- Hold people accountable
- Inspire internal motivation
- Lead by example
- Manage a project
- Encourage innovation
- Manage change
- Monitor progress
- Deal with mistakes
- Recognize achievement
- Reinforce expectations
- Conduct performance review
- Facilitate idea generation
- Evaluate ethical factors
- Facilitate thinking
- Facilitate conflict resolution

- Facilitate decision making
- Involve people in decisions
- Manage a crisis
- Conduct a meeting
- Facilitate cooperation
- Facilitate team bonding

People skills are one of the biggest "difference-makers" in the workplace. The difference between a leader and a manager is people skills. The difference between a good employee and a stronger, high-performing employee is people skills. That's why year after year executives rank "people skills" at the top of their wish lists when hiring people.

Chapter 7

Personal Strengths are Core Strengths

Years ago I was talking with a CEO about leadership skills. Here's what he told me: "It's not what you know. It's not what you can do. It's who you are."

These high-sounding words seemed to have the ring of truth. But I expressed my reservations. "Yes, you have to be strong as a person, but how will the world know who the leader is until he manifests it in what he does?"

We agreed to disagree. But now, 20 years later, I see that we were both right. Who you are is at the core of your strength and effectiveness. It's terribly important. But this core isn't about passive traits, values, virtues or attributes. It's about observable behavior patterns. In the end, an individual has to act. One has to actually do the hard things.

Also at the core – personal strengths

When I was a young lieutenant, I attended three months of training at the Army Ranger School, where I learned a lot of difficult combat skills. I learned how to navigate for miles at night through dense underbrush up and down mountains in order to reach a distant objective before dawn. I learned how to lead an infantry attack while coordinating medical evacuations, artillery fire and air strikes—all at the same time. You get the picture.

I got good at it. And when I arrived in Vietnam, I was glad I had these skills. But I learned something important. Performing in combat is so adverse that none of these combat skills are worth much if you can't be bold, keep your cool, manage your awareness, be flexible, give maximum effort, exercise judgment and yes, even show compassion. The biggest challenge was exercising these personal strengths, not the combat skills.

I've been intensely interested in these core strengths ever since. In April 1999 I published an article in *Performance Improvement*, "Strengths of Character: A New Dimension of Human Performance." The paradigm in the HRD world at the time held that competence consisted of skills and knowledge. I made a case that a third element, which I called "character strength," was also a factor. As usual, very few professionals actually read the article, and it had virtually no impact. No splash, no ripples.

But you know I'm right about this. You can have abundant knowledge and a high level of skill. But what if conditions turn against you? What if you encounter opposition? What if things go wrong? What if the stakes are raised and the cost of failure is multiplied? What if you're getting pressure from stakeholders? What if office politics gets in your way? What if customers are angry about problems? What if the competition has introduced something new and powerful? What if three members of your team have left for other opportunities? What if your child is diagnosed with a rare form of cancer?

The answer is, you'll have to do some hard things. And what you actually do will be a manifestation of who you are, at the core.

Personal strengths include character strengths – and more

As I said, I used to talk about this in terms of "character." But the more I studied this topic, the more I realized that there's little agreement as to what character is. Every model I've studied is different. The "Character Counts" movement has six pillars, and their approach is to teach it in the classroom. The best book on the subject is *Character Strengths and Virtues: A Handbook and Classification,* by Christopher Peterson and Martin Seligman (Oxford, 2004). This thoroughly academic approach has 24 virtues in its model. Some models I've seen have over 100.

I was troubled by the fact that none of the models portray character strengths as behavior patterns. Perhaps this is why the proponents of these models believe that study and classroom instruction will have an impact on a person's character development. Furthermore, there are important behavior patterns that aren't mentioned in any of the models, such as proactivity, thoroughness, self-esteem, loyalty and others. Because of these issues, I decided that referring to these behavior patterns as character strengths would create barriers to understanding.

This is why I now refer to them as "personal strengths." Yes, many of the personal strengths include the same character strengths that are part of various models. But I feel it's important to go beyond these models to be more inclusive and establish this aspect of "who you are" as core elements of behavior.

In other words, you're honest only if in your behavior you routinely tell the truth. You're compassionate only if in your behavior you routinely avoid hurting people, if you take their feelings into account.

When the going gets rough, actions count more than anything. And the most effective actions are almost never easy. That's why I prefer to call them "strengths."

I once knew a brilliant lawyer who had a drinking problem. As his habit got worse, he was no longer sober by mid-afternoon. It affected his work. Fortunately, his family and partners confronted him and he entered into rehab, where he gained self-awareness and learned self-discipline. He had the personal strength to change his behavior, and he's been a wonderful husband and father and a successful lawyer ever since.

Personal strengths are a key factor in performance

One of my friends in high school went into the Air Force. It was during the early years of the Vietnam War, and he was quickly promoted to sergeant. But he had severe self-esteem and honesty issues. When his alcohol and drug addictions were discovered, he was dishonorably discharged, which only made matters worse. He was smart and could have succeeded in life, but he had integrity and loyalty issues. His core weaknesses made him unfit for most work. He moved to Miami, where he could get drugs more easily. I assume he lied to the wrong people, because he was later found murdered.

Why did the able, experienced and well-positioned business executive Bernie Madoff become the poster-monster for a lack of integrity? In spite of his education and business expertise, for over 20 years he misled thousands of wealthy investors using a massive Ponzi scheme to defraud them of over $60 billion. This set some kind of world record for "breaking trust." His deception was not only a colossal example of a lack of integrity, it was a felony—several felonies. Instead of using his considerable business acumen to make a difference, he's been convicted and sentenced to 150 years in prison and is now serving the equivalent of a life sentence at a medium-security federal prison in Butner, North Carolina.

This is an extreme example, but there are thousands. No doubt you can easily recall someone who was limited not by ability, motivation or empowerment, but by deficits of personal strength. And these examples illustrate only a few of the personal strengths. The list below displays the 40 strength areas currently supported by our online self-development service, *Strong for Performance*:

- Acceptance
- Accountability
- Awareness
- Commitment
- Compassion
- Composure
- Cooperation
- Courage
- Creativity
- Decisiveness
- Effort
- Empowerment
- Excellence
- Fairness
- Flexibility
- Focus
- Gratitude
- Honesty

- Initiative
- Integrity
- Intuition
- Loyalty
- Open-mindedness
- Optimism
- Passion
- Patience
- Perseverance
- Proactivity
- Rationality
- Responsibility
- Self-awareness
- Self-confidence
- Self-development
- Self-discipline
- Self-esteem
- Service
- Thoroughness
- Tolerance
- Trust
- Vision

Some important "bottom lines" about personal strengths:

- **Of all the elements of performance, personal strengths probably have the greatest impact.** "Who you are" really is that significant. Imagine someone who lacked business know-how but was strong in most aspects of personal strength. Lack of business know-how can be remedied and expertise can be developed in a relatively short period of time. But the consequences of deficits in personal strength are enormous.

- **Personal strengths *can* be developed.** For most people, some strengths are developed in youth. This kind of development can and should continue indefinitely, using opportunities to strive against adversity and learning from these experiences.

- **Personal strengths are poorly understood.** The notion of "character strength" has always been a foggy one, and it has never been understood as a crucial element of workplace performance. Consequently, it's never been recognized as something you can develop in leaders and high-performing employees.

And that's unfortunate, because like people skills, you can help people strengthen the behavior patterns that define "who they are." And if employees don't manifest these personal strengths, you'll never get the kind of results you want from them.

Chapter 8

Connecting the Dots

$50 billion down a hole? $100 billion? For no gain? Every year? Whichever figure you believe, it seems to me that it qualifies as "big bucks." Wasting that much money is a scandal.

It's important—for you—that you don't go into denial about this, thinking that somehow you're immune, that what you're doing is special and not susceptible to the realities of learning and development.

If you care about the bottom line, you care about how well people do their jobs. So you've probably invested in their development. And I wonder: *how much money are you pouring down that hole?*

The reason I've written this, why I'm not politely mincing words, is because I really want you to acknowledge the four realities. A lot rides on your doing this. You can't eliminate training programs. Even the best people come to you unprepared for what challenges them, needing more knowledge and more skills. Training will always be essential, and it will never come cheap. The point is, you want this training to "stick." You really do want their behavior to change. You want results—a huge return on all this money you're investing in training.

If you've read this far, you now understand the four realities.

Reality #1

Most of the money invested in learning and development is wasted.

Only a fraction of what you spend on training actually changes behavior.

Reality #2

At work, people usually don't think about how to act; instead, they automatically engage ingrained work habits.

Because people won't use a skill consistently until it's ingrained.

Reality #3

To ingrain a work habit, people have to rewire their brains—they have to apply the skill over and over until the related brain cells connect into a new neural pathway, a process that takes far more time than is available in a training program.

Ingraining a new skill or work habit requires a lot of follow-through repetition.

Reality #4

Employees need people skills and personal strengths to work at their best.

Business, administrative, management and technical skills are only part of the performance equation.

Knowledge isn't the same as skill. Knowing what to do doesn't automatically lead to doing it. What happens in training can be an excellent beginning, but it's ***only the beginning.*** If you want people to consistently apply the best practice models they learn about in the classroom, they need to apply the models in the workplace over and over for months afterward. This is because work habits are ingrained over time after persistent repetition. Months of reinforcement, application, feedback, encouragement and accountability are needed for people to consistently do what you want them to do on the job.

Yes, there are the rare individuals—the self-motivated high-performers and life-long learners who are so obsessed with achievement and success that they coach themselves. They perform the desired behaviors on the job and keep after it in spite of failure and frustration until they ultimately ingrain the skills—whether you have an adequate follow-through program or not. But most people will need a structured system of support during the long journey towards "unconscious competence."

And finally, people have to be strong at the core to achieve the results you expect of them. They need to continuously improve their *people skills* and build up *personal strengths*.

The problem is, the HR world has done a better job of sounding the alarm than it has of helping you put out the fire. That's why I was reluctant to write my "dark secret" article in the first place. And that's why I wouldn't blame you if you said, "It's too hard. Screw it. I already have plenty of other issues to deal with."

But before you dismiss this "heads-up" I've given you, let me outline a basic approach that will fix all these issues.

Chapter 9

What It Takes to Make Training Stick

Recognizing the lack of consensus about solutions to this horrible problem, I decided to consolidate the confusing array of recommendations into a practical, coherent strategy. In 2007 I published a 16-page monograph in the *ASTD Infoline* series, entitled "Enhance the Transfer of Training." In it I reaffirmed the problem, explained why follow-through was absolutely essential to ingraining newly learned skills, and outlined a practical approach for making training "stick."

Unfortunately, like all the previous articles and books about transfer of training, my paper was just one more tree that fell in the woods with no one around to hear it. The message never reached top management.

A bottom-line approach to making training "stick"

Nevertheless, the document is still available. You can download it from our website at http://www.prostarcoach.com/articles.htm. I encourage you to read it. In it I outlined eight initiatives, which I summarize here:

Focus on shortcomings. The basic principle: don't invest in training if there's not a deficit in vital skills or knowledge. "Vital" means that the deficit is what's causing your failure to achieve a major business goal. A traditional HR "needs assessment" won't do the job. You have to start by identifying which of your key business results are falling short, then find out what's causing the shortfall. Is the problem with a specific area of your organization? Does the problem there have to do with a deficit in skills or knowledge? Or is it being caused by something else?

Set up training transfer. A lot can happen in the classroom. A lot of trainers believe training needs to be fun. If you were to audit some of their instruction, you might see media that motivate attendees to value the content, as well as exercises designed to make key points.

But the meat of a training program is when a best practice skill is explained and lots of time is devoted to simulated practice. Also essential to setting up transfer of the training is to give job aids of the model to participants so they can refer to them in the workplace. Smart trainers also introduce a post-instruction program of follow-through reinforcement and accountability exercises.

Coordinate learning networks. In training at its best, people learn from each other, as well as from the instructors. They observe each other's practice and give feedback, insights and tips. Ideally, this kind of coaching should continue after training. Typically, many people care whether an individual is improving workplace skills: managers, mentors, co-participants, colleagues and direct reports. These are valuable sources of input, feedback, encouragement and accountability as a person tries to ingrain what was learned in training. You can make these interactions happen by structuring learning relationships and the use of communication media for this purpose.

Prepare coaches. The most valuable coaching resource is an individual's manager. The problem is, managers are chosen mostly for their business and technical expertise, not for their leadership skills. Even if you invest in leadership training, you may not be giving managers coaching skills. This failure is a huge lost opportunity.

Integrate follow-up. Often, diagnostic assessment is integrated with the training programs. Assessment can diagnose skill deficiencies and other performance issues. This can help determine which training should be conducted. Assessment is also useful after training to determine whether performance is improving. These are excellent trends, but practically no one is adding follow-through reinforcement, application, feedback, coaching, and encouragement to this system.

Insist on accountability. The best way to hold people accountable is to measure their ability to do what they're supposed to do—before and at several intervals after training. Then you can compare the measurements to evaluate progress. Everyone involved in the performance improvement effort can be held accountable by this data—the learner, the trainers and the manager.

Align culture. If you were to try to implement all of the above into a system of follow-through, what barriers would stand in your way? Modify your policies and practices to support ongoing performance improvement.

Gain commitment. All of this probably adds up to more than a few changes in the way people are trained and led. You'll need to exercise leadership to get people to understand and support all these changes.

It won't be easy...

I'll be the first to admit that this approach asks you to do a lot. Right now, no organization in the world is set up to provide the kind of follow-up support learners need to ingrain skills over time.

For example, I say that people need coaching. And they do! Even elite professional athletes need coaching. Why would your employees be any different? You might hire coaches for top executives, but you'll go broke providing coaches for all your managers, let alone your employees.

That's why I say the best approach is to upgrade the coaching skills of your managers and require them to use these skills. After all, it's their job to develop, inspire and empower their direct reports. It would make a big difference if they enriched their leadership toolkit with a few good coaching skills. Still, this initiative would require additional leadership development training for most of them.

I talk about learning networks—colleagues helping each other learn. People learn best from experience on the job, and a variety of people care whether they do that. Bosses, mentors and peer coaches can offer their experience, feedback, encouragement and accountability. But how do you set this up? Email? Forums? Instant messaging? Lunch-and-learn sessions? How would you structure this to make it work? What technology supports this kind of interaction?

We say that assessment and training programs need to be integrated with follow-through reinforcement—a single system of ongoing performance improvement. This means you should evaluate skill levels before training and then at regular intervals afterward to check progress. Done right, this can hold people accountable for improvement. Does your in-house assessment technology make this easy? Does *any* assessment technology?

And what about training everyone in the core people skills? There are dozens of people skills. This sounds like an ongoing effort—a big expense.

And "personal strengths." These may be the core abilities of leaders and high performers, but it's possible that before reading this book you never heard of personal strength. You've heard of character strength, and you know how important it is. Even so, if you wanted to help develop your employees in this area, how would you go about it? How do you train stuff like this?

Practically speaking, the simplest possible solution won't be simple to implement—if you want it to work. You could challenge your HR experts to create the systems, platforms and technologies to support all this. But does it make sense that every organization diverts precious resources to create their unique home-grown systems? Why haven't the experts figured this out? Where's the technology to support all this?

These are valid questions, the ones that ultimately drove us to create **Strong for Performance**. But evolving that technology was a story in itself.

Chapter 10

Why We Created Strong for Performance

Strong for Performance is a highly innovative online virtual coaching system, a self-development subscription service that supports the ongoing reinforcement, application, feedback, encouragement and accountability needed to ingrain skills over the long haul.

This program is so different from conventional goal-setting programs, learning management systems, or talent management systems that when learning professionals first learn about it, they aren't sure what it is. I like to call it a learning empowerment system.

A technology that supports follow-through

Years ago, when we talked with our colleagues and customers about the massive amount of post-training follow-through required to go from knowing to doing, they said they didn't have the technology to support it. At the time there was no system that addressed the real issues. They would need a completely new kind of technology.

We believed that if we could create a service that did this, while actually helping them change people's behavior, the vision of our company would be fulfilled and we would benefit as a business.

We first began working on the concept early in 2004. But the true story of its development is linked to the history of 360-degree feedback and *20/20 Insight*, our multi-functional feedback survey.

Back in the mid-80s, 360-degree feedback was still a new concept. It was expensive—about $250 per recipient (in 1980s dollars). So it was mostly considered an executive development service, and nearly all the assessments focused on a proprietary set of "researched" leadership and management behaviors—often more than 100 items. This was a challenge for feedback responders, and the process was difficult to administer. Because executives weren't used to receiving feedback about their leadership from direct reports, they were anxious before, during and after the process. The feedback reports were filled with so much data that a trained facilitator was needed to help executives make use of it.

So in 1994 we introduced **20/20 Insight**, a multi-functional survey tool. It's optimized for 360-degree feedback, and when we released it we positioned it as such. Our vision was to change the industry's approach to feedback surveys. Feedback is an essential first step towards professional development, and every employee in the organization needs it, not just top management. The flexibility of **20/20 Insight** made this possible.

It changed the game. It was an onsite administration software, not a central administration service. The software made it easy for organizations to customize the surveys in its feedback library so the items could be validated for local conditions. Because administering multi-source feedback can be a complex undertaking, we made the process an intuitive "no-brainer."

This wasn't the first time we challenged existing HR paradigms, and we knew we had a lot of explaining to do. But our approach made sense, and executives were quick to catch on. Before we knew it, other 360-degree feedback providers were taking a similar approach. With the arrival of the world-wide web and the 21st century, several dozen variations of this service became available. By then, nearly every organization of any size had used 360 technology.

360-degree feedback is the only practical way to measure the most important component of leader and team performance—people skills and personal strengths. But like training, *360-degree feedback—by itself—isn't a cure for performance problems*. Knowing what the shortfalls are is only the first step. The next step is to find out the reasons for the shortfalls. And if know-how is the issue, then training may be appropriate.

Our early attempts to support follow-through

As I've emphasized throughout this book, *assessment and training—by themselves —cannot change a person's behavior.* A lot has to happen after assessment or after training to help a person ingrain the desired changes in behavior.

Intuitively, we appreciated this in the early 1990s, so we included post-assessment follow-through resources with the earliest versions of *20/20 Insight*. We built specific developmental recommendations into the feedback reports. And each participant received a booklet called *Development Planning Guide*. In 1995, this was replaced by a software program called *Individual Development Planner* (IDP), which helped a participant analyze the causes for performance issues, plan developmental actions, and track progress.

In 1996 we added the *360 SmartKit* to guide administrators and facilitators in the use of these resources. With the advent of the web, we moved most of *20/20 Insight's* functions and resources online. The *360 Smart Kit* was updated and moved to the web as *20/20 PowerUser*.

Our users then began asking for an online version of IDP, but we had expanded our knowledge of how skills are ingrained and the kind of follow-through that was needed. We saw that IDP had been a fine beginning but its functions would fall far short of what was needed. So instead of investing in an online version of IDP, as an interim measure in 2004 we published an updated digital workbook called *Self-Development Toolkit*. To enlighten executives and HR professionals about the need for follow-through, we also distributed an eBook called *Train-to-Ingrain*.

During all this we asked our *20/20 Insight* users, affiliates and consultants for ideas about an ideal replacement for IDP. We asked them to think creatively, and we collected dozens of ideas. We had been thinking about an online individual development service since 2004, and their ideas fed this concept.

As we considered the science of learning and what it takes to transfer knowledge in the classroom to performance in the workplace, we realized that the kind of support an organization would need would be a whole lot more than our associates imagined.

This is why, in 2007, we began designing and developing what came to be called **Strong for Performance**.

One of the exciting things that happens when you develop a new product is that the process teaches you about the product you're working on. So innovations evolve beyond what we imagined they would be.

Chapter 11

Virtual Coaching and the Coaching Network

After training is over, what people need most is coaching: reinforcement, feedback, application, encouragement and accountability. A lot of it. The consistent, repeated application that's needed to ingrain a new work habit usually takes months. Without coaching, the chances that someone will persist in spite of the inevitable setbacks and discouragement are slim.

So, you have a problem. Who's going to do all this coaching?

You're not going to pay for executive coaching for everyone you send to training. You can't afford it. No one can. This is why in my 2007 *ASTD Infoline* article I suggested that you empower your managers to coach their direct reports—a reasonable enrichment of their leadership roles. But as I pointed out earlier, this is not a simple solution to your coaching problem.

We develop a coaching technology that supports behavior change

Many managers don't accept the idea that it's their job to help direct reports grow in their jobs. Most of the books on coaching are addressed to mentors or professional coaches, not managers. Only one or two acknowledge that managers should have coaching skills. Off-the-shelf training packages focus more on coaching-related motivation and knowledge, rather than specific coaching skills.

As we began creating *Strong for Performance*, helping you deal with this challenge became our mission. At first we phrased our opportunity this way:

What if we could create a technology that helps managers, trainers, consultants and even professional coaches become better coaches?

Soon after that, we expanded our vision of what was possible:

What if we could create a multi-faceted virtual coaching system that provides excellent developmental coaching and changed behavior with or without the help of these professionals?

To make a long story short, that's what we did. ***Strong for Performance*** is a virtual coaching system unlike anything that exists today. Each participant receives a one-year subscription with 24/7 access to a suite of several breakthrough learning technologies, all of which contribute virtual coaching in various forms.

The program has a special interface for an administrator (HR professional, trainer or consultant) to set up links to your own training content, such as articles, exercises, graphics, PowerPoint files, videos and podcasts. These reinforcing references are easily accessed in the ***Strong for Performance*** program, empowering long-term follow-through after training.

In addition to your custom content, *Strong for Performance* has a vast library of rich content focused on people skills and personal strengths. People skills videos present step-by-step how-to instructions for performing each skill. Over two dozen people skills are represented. The videos are supplemented by audio files and job aids. Each video is linked to a coaching exercise that guides the participant to reflect on main points.

Personal strength resources consist of seven types of media exercises available to ingrain 40 different personal strengths. Participants engage in self-directed learning based on their learning styles and priority focus. They are coached to understand and apply the content in the workplace.

The *Strong for Performance* program coaches participants to ingrain core strength behavior patterns through cycles of *Focus*, *Action* and *Reflection (FAR)*. Based on self-awareness or feedback, individuals *focus* on a single skill or strength. After absorbing content related to this area, they complete an exercise that concludes with a "***planned action***," an intention to apply an aspect of what was learned.

After this workplace application, the participant completes a follow-up "***reflection exercise***," which draws out lessons learned from the experience and next steps. This focus-action-reflection cycle is then repeated indefinitely until the new behavior pattern becomes automatic.

The Coaching Network

To supplement the built-in elements of virtual coaching, ***Strong for Performance*** has a unique feature called the "Coaching Network," a private forum where real people support an individual's efforts to improve. Participants recruit a network of support coaches, people who care about the person's growth and success: co-participants in training, direct reports, coworkers, managers, mentors, trainers, consultants, professional coaches, even friends and family. One person will serve as their **accountability coach** to ensure they implement the actions they commit to.

When a user completes an exercise, it is saved in a confidential area called the "Learning

Archive," and Coaching Network members can be asked for their input about these exercises and other learning activities.

Another dimension of coaching is feedback. The "Get Feedback" feature enables *diagnostic* feedback, which helps a person choose an area to work on, and *focused* feedback, which helps a person measure progress in a particular area. Both diagnostic feedback and focused feedback also gather "feedforward," which collects suggestions for performing more effectively in the future. Users have the option to self-assess and compare their ratings with those from others.

Most of the time when you hear the term "virtual coaching," it refers to professional coaches who communicate through the internet rather than in person or by phone. ***Strong for Performance*** goes far beyond this to provide something really unique—true multi-faceted virtual coaching that reinforces, coordinates feedback, encourages and establishes accountability.

We designed ***Strong for Performance*** to be refreshingly easy on HR support staff, because it requires no training of the participants. It's an intuitive system, and how-to media are built-in. More important, it's loaded with content, so it develops people without them having to leave their desk, an important consideration in tough economic times.

If you'd like details or a guided tour, visit **http://www.StrongForPerformance.com** or call (800-488-6463 or 757-873-3700) or email (info@prostarcoach.com).

What could be better than *Strong for Performance?* We've asked ourselves that question, and the answer we came up with is outlined in the final chapter.

Chapter 12

Your Future Employees: Individual Achievers and Rising Stars

Strong for Performance solves the problem of follow-through reinforcement and coaching. It's the kind of system you'll want in place all the time—to reinforce and ingrain the skills your employees learned about in training and to constantly improve their core people skills and personal strengths.

But wouldn't it be great if the people you were hiring already had strong people skills and personal strengths?

Virtual coaching for your future employees

For this reason, we developed another version of this system, called ***Strong for Life***, for young people who aren't working for you yet—high school or college students who are about to enter the workforce. ***Strong for Life*** is designed for young people to self-develop *autonomously*.

Start growing winners when they're teens

Strong for Life is not just for the best students, but also for those involved in student government, athletic high-performers, community contributors and self-starters who are working multiple jobs or starting small businesses. Instead of waiting until these success-oriented people enter the world of work, *Strong for Life* can help them build core people skills and personal strengths while their lives are still mostly involved in learning.

Help them develop vital critical thinking skills

Young people need *Strong for Life* for another, equally important reason. This is the period in their life when the prefrontal cortex (PFC) is developing. This is a rather large area of the brain located right behind the forehead. In my opinion, this time represents the most critical phase of brain development. While the rest of the brain handles "what is," the PFC handles "what things mean" and imagining what could be.

The PFC, often called the "executive" part of the brain, processes intuition and logic, cause-and-effect understanding, foresight and planning. These functions enable self-management and analytical thinking. Along with language, PFC thinking is what makes human beings smarter than other animals. More than any other part of the brain, the PFC contributes to a person's success in the world. And yet, the developmental process itself can be upsetting and can easily go awry.

Scientists now know that PFC brain development begins at puberty. So the years from 12 to 24 are the critical period during which a young person "uses or loses" PFC brain cells. Only the PFC brain cells that are used repeatedly during youth survive and become the foundation for conceptual thinking during the rest of adult life. More learning will be possible after that, but the platform for this will be limited to the size of the already established foundation.

But there's a problem. The development of brain cells in the PFC temporarily disrupts a young person's ability to reason and self-manage, making it difficult to reinforce this kind of thinking. At a time when teenagers' bodies are upset by hormonal growth, new body sensations and strong emotions, they are singularly ill-equipped to understand what's happening to them and to manage their impulses. Later, if the PFC has developed normally, they'll be better able to deal with all that. But exercising the PFC during youth is like asking them to pull themselves up by their own bootstraps.

Young people are unlikely to make the most of this confusing time of life without help. Three things are needed. First, adults have to maintain trusting relationships with the young person. This means unconditional love, understanding, role modeling, communication, patience and encouragement. In other words, if the teenager's erratic behavior provokes a hostile reaction from adults, the result will be alienation and the so-called "generation gap." This all-too-frequent relationship disaster means that the teen won't heed even the best coaching.

While young people are having trouble controlling their emotions and impulses, trusted adults can provide boundaries, structure, understanding and coaching.

Supportive adults need to encourage adolescents to think for themselves. Questions like, "Why do you think this happened?" and "If you do this, what do you think will happen next?" and "What do you think you should do differently next time?" cause a young person to engage the PFC. The more they try to understand, reason through problems, control their emotions, imagine cause and effect, and focus on goal achievement, the more extensively PFC networks will establish themselves during this critical time of life.

Adolescence - a huge turning point in life

The window of opportunity for PFC brain cell development *opens* at puberty and *closes* in the early twenties. Everyone knows this is a difficult time of life, but almost no one knows how high the stakes are. The lucky kids are the ones who have parents, teachers and coaches who can coach and encourage them. These relationships determine whether a teenager will grow up equipped to pursue being a doctor, a lawyer, an executive, an engineer, a scientist, or other professional careers.

Or, if the youth is alienated and follows his or her emotional and biological impulses, then the individual may get into trouble with addictions, illegal activity, gangs, pregnancy, accidents or even suicide. The young people who waste the opportunity of the teenage years will advance into adult life with limited intellectual capacity.

Strong for Life is uniquely designed to give young people this kind of PFC stimulation and development, along with core skills and strengths that will prepare them to be successful in life. Our vision is to put this program in the hands of hundreds of thousands of young adults every year.

So while you're taking care of developing the people who carry out your mission, we'll be doing our best to develop the people who will carry out your mission in the future.

It takes a village...

As we developed *Strong for Life*, we realized that in the best case many adults get involved in raising a child to be an effective adult, not just the parents: relatives, teachers, athletic coaches, youth program leaders and other mentors.

The problem is, as I explained earlier, that most adults don't have the best communication skills, and it takes these skills to mentor youth effectively.

So we developed a family of online virtual coaching systems to help adult mentors improve their coaching skills:

- ***Strong for Parenting*** (for parents and relatives)
- ***Strong for Mentoring Students*** (for teachers)
- ***Strong for Mentoring Athletes*** (for coaches)
- ***Strong for Mentoring Youth*** (for youth program leaders)

To learn more about these systems, visit **http://www.ProStarCoach.com**.

Chapter 13

Are You Ready to Ask the Hard Questions?

Imagine this:

*Everyone in your organization checks their **Strong for Performance** interface for a few minutes every day. They understand the importance of people skills and personal strengths, and they know that the journey of getting stronger in these areas never really ends. Everyone has their own individual self-development focus, and administrators monitor usage of **Strong for Performance** and check progress. Through the Coaching Network, employees support each other as peer coaches—people who care about their success. Training is conducted to correct competence issues related to shortfalls in business results.*

These instructional events are the first step in a long-term program of follow-through in the workplace—application, feedback, reinforcement, coaching, accountability and encouragement until newly learned skills are ingrained. Success stories of people making lasting changes in behavior—once rare—are now commonplace. Learning is now considered a part of work, not a classroom activity. This approach has become part of your culture, and you turn away consultants who aren't aligned with it.

Everything you've read in this document points to this vision. It's a realistic, technology-supported vision of learning and development that actually produces the lasting changes in behavior and improvements in performance you want to pay for.

A lot depends on whether you're ready to ask some hard questions. If you've acknowledged the realities of learning I've presented here, then a reasonable next step will be to consider your own organization.

- How much do you invest to improve the abilities of the people you hire?
- Are managers good at coaching people to get better at what they do?
- Do they understand the importance of core people skills and personal strengths to achieving these levels of performance?
- Are people in your organization working on improving people skills and personal strengths?
- Do you systematically measure performance to find out whether skills have improved several months after training?
- What happens after training? After instruction, do participants get involved in a structured, long-term program to ingrain newly learned skills? Exactly what kind of follow-through is going on?
- How confident are you that the money you spend on training actually translates to lasting changes in behavior and improvements in performance? Are you really getting the payoff you expect when you invest in training?

You can spend an awful lot of money on learning management systems, training technology, corporate universities, off-the-shelf programs, advanced talent management systems, consultants and guest speakers. Everything can be state-of-the-art and the best that money can buy. But that doesn't mean that any of this will—by itself—improve people's behavior patterns.

Realistically, it's a matter of cause and effect. If your employees don't repeatedly apply what they've learned, the brain cells involved in those actions won't connect into circuits, skills will never be ingrained, and what they learned will rarely be used in the workplace.

You *can* get what you want from training. You actually *can* get people to change the way they perform every day, if you have a structured program of long-term follow-through coaching and reinforcement. You *can* help your employees become stronger to meet the challenges of work—and their lives.

Strong for Performance was designed to support your efforts to make this happen. You can learn more about it at **http://www.StrongForPerformance.com**.

Dennis E. Coates, Ph.D.

CEO and Co-founder of Performance Support Systems, Inc.

Denny has been a human resources development professional for over 35 years. All his work has been about pursuing two questions. How do people learn - how does it really happen in the brain? And what can people learn that will make the biggest difference in their work and lives?

Denny has been CEO of Performance Support Systems, Inc., since 1987. In 1988 he developed *MindFrames*, a personality assessment based on cognitive neuroscience. In 1994 he created *20/20 Insight*, an online multi-source survey platform. Since then it has been used by hundreds of organizations worldwide to assess and develop managers and employees.

Denny is also the creator of **Strong for Performance** and several related online virtual coaching programs for developing personal strengths and people skills. Over the years, his programs have helped millions of people grow stronger for the challenges of work and life. These days he spends most of his time writing about personal development, communication skills, personal strength and parenting teens.